ALEXANDER HAMILTON

BOOK FOR CURIOUS KIDS

Exploring the Fascinating Life Story of the Orphan Who Became a Founding Father

MARK LYLANI

TABLE OF CONTENTS

INTRODUCTION

What drives a man to rise from obscurity to shape a nation's destiny? How does a boy born on a remote Caribbean island overcome abandonment, poverty, and personal tragedy to become one of the most influential figures in American history? What can we learn from his relentless ambition, intellectual brilliance, and passionate vision for a new country?

These questions lie at the heart of Alexander Hamilton's extraordinary life story. His journey, from his humble beginnings on the island of Nevis to his pivotal role in the American Revolution and the formation of the United States, is a testament to resilience, ingenuity, and unyielding determination. But who was Alexander Hamilton beyond the famed statesman depicted in history books and celebrated on Broadway?

This book delves into Alexander Hamilton's multifaceted life, exploring his profound impact on America's early political landscape, his visionary economic policies, and the personal struggles that shaped his character. From his childhood on the islands to his tragic duel in Weehawken, we follow Hamilton's path through pivotal moments in history, revealing the complexities and contradictions of a man who left an indelible mark on the nation.

As you journey through these pages, consider: How did Hamilton's early experiences with loss and hardship inform his relentless pursuit of success? What motivated his passionate advocacy for a strong central government and economic modernization? And in the face of scandal and rivalry, how did he navigate the treacherous waters of early American politics?

Hamilton's life is not just a chronicle of achievements but a story of ambition, conflict, and legacy. His ideas and contributions continue to resonate, prompting reflection on the enduring principles that underpin the American experiment. Join us in exploring the life of Alexander Hamilton, a founding father whose legacy still shapes the United States today.

The Boy from the Islands

Alexander Hamilton was born in 1755 on the small island of Nevis in the West Indies. Although the exact date of his birth remains uncertain, it is traditionally recorded as January 11.

When Alexander was a young child, his father, James Hamilton, abandoned the family, leaving his mother, Rachel Faucette Lavien, to care for him and his brother, James. Despite facing significant financial hardships, she was resolute in her effort to provide her sons with a quality education and worked tirelessly to keep them in school.

From an early age, Hamilton exhibited a voracious appetite for learning. He read extensively and maximized the limited resources available, often borrowing books. His writing skills impressed not only his teachers but also community members.

Tragedy struck in 1768 when Rachel died from a severe illness, leaving Alexander orphaned at the tender age of thirteen. This adversity only strengthened his determination to succeed, aware that his future depended heavily on his own efforts and abilities.

Recognizing his potential, local businessmen and community leaders facilitated his move to New York City in 1772 for further education. Their financial support enabled Hamilton to enroll at King's College.

Upon arriving in New York, Hamilton entered an environment starkly different from his native Nevis. The city's vibrant intellectual and political life immediately captivated him, and he swiftly became an ardent supporter of the revolutionary cause. His college experiences crucially shaped his path toward advocating for independence from Great Britain.

Hamilton rapidly distinguished himself, joining a local militia as tensions in the colonies escalated. His eloquence and commanding presence marked him as a notable figure in the early stages of the American Revolution.

This journey from a boy on a small Caribbean island to a key figure in bustling New York represents just the beginning of Alexander Hamilton's significant impact. He went on to become a Founding Father of the United

States, playing critical roles both during and after the revolution.

The subsequent chapters will delve into Hamilton's substantial contributions to the American Revolution and the founding of the nation, including his pivotal role in crafting the United States Constitution. His enduring legacy continues to shape the fabric of American society today.

A Life Altered

In this chapter, we delve into a pivotal period in Alexander Hamilton's life—a series of events that dramatically shaped his destiny.

Born on January 11, 1755, on the Caribbean island of Nevis, Alexander was the son of James Hamilton, a Scottish trader, and Rachel Faucette Lavien, of French Huguenot descent.

Tragedy struck repeatedly during Alexander's early years. His father abandoned the family, which compromised their financial stability. At around the age of 13, Alexander's life took another devastating turn when his mother died of yellow fever, leaving him and his brother James orphaned and facing a highly uncertain future.

Following his mother's death, a cousin briefly took in the brothers, but after the cousin's subsequent suicide, Alexander found himself under the care of Thomas Stevens, a local merchant.

Despite these adversities, Alexander's resolve did not waver. He developed an insatiable thirst for knowledge, reading extensively and learning the intricacies of commerce while working at a mercantile business. He was fortunate to receive guidance from local businessmen who recognized his sharp intellect and mentored him.

Alexander's keen intelligence and determination were noticed by the influential members of his community in Nevis. After writing a detailed account of a hurricane that had ravaged the islands, local businessmen sponsored his journey to the North American colonies for further education.

In 1772, Alexander left the Caribbean behind and arrived in Elizabethtown, New Jersey. He attended a preparatory school there, preparing himself for college. This move marked his entry into a world filled with new opportunities, educational prospects, and the beginnings of his political journey.

He later enrolled at King's College in New York City, where he studied a variety of subjects that fueled his interest in political theory and practice. His academic excellence and eloquent writings drew the attention of revolutionary leaders and immersed him in significant political dialogues.

Alexander Hamilton's early struggles and experiences paved the way for his transformation from a destitute orphan to a prominent figure in America's fight for independence. His exceptional intelligence, unyielding pursuit of knowledge, and active political engagement laid the groundwork for his future achievements as one of the founding fathers of the United States.

Journey to the Colonies

After enduring the personal tragedies of his father's abandonment and his mother's death, Alexander Hamilton was left to fend for himself as a young boy on the Caribbean island of Nevis. Despite these adversities, his life was poised for a dramatic shift toward an extraordinary future.

Carrying responsibilities far beyond his years, Hamilton made a pivotal decision as a teenager. He left the Caribbean to seek a new beginning in the American colonies. His driving force was a desire for educational opportunities unavailable in his homeland. He managed to secure passage on a ship bound for North America.

The voyage was marred by rough seas, causing Hamilton considerable seasickness. Nevertheless, he remained resilient, recognizing that overcoming these challenges was crucial to accessing the opportunities that awaited him in the American colonies.

Upon arrival in New York, Hamilton was immediately captivated by the vibrant atmosphere and potential of this bustling city. However, as an immigrant and a financially unsupported youth, he quickly understood the necessity of working diligently to establish himself in this new environment.

Determined to advance, Hamilton found employment and pursued his education. Working as a clerk and juggling other jobs, he connected with local businessmen and intellectuals. This period marked the beginning of Hamilton's passion for writing and his engagement in political discourse. His quick intellect and thirst for knowledge allowed him to become a self-taught scholar in economics and governance.

Hamilton's articulate writing and sharp intellect gained the attention of influential New Yorkers, leading to a scholarship at King's College. There, his talents flourished even further.

While at King's College, Hamilton actively participated in the rising political debates, vocally advocating for colonial independence. This stance earned him both admiration and notoriety. His influential writings and speeches during this period laid the foundation for his future role as a key figure in U.S. history.

Influenced by Enlightenment thinkers such as John Locke, Hamilton's political philosophy was deeply shaped by ideas of liberty, social contracts, and government. These concepts profoundly influenced his thoughts and writings, which later became fundamental to shaping the nation.

Thus, Hamilton's journey to the colonies was not only a physical relocation but also a transformative path of personal and intellectual growth. Starting from humble beginnings on a small Caribbean island, Hamilton embraced the challenges and opportunities of his new life, rising to become a central figure in America's fight for independence and good governance.

Fighting for Freedom

In the early 1770s, Alexander Hamilton, a young, intellectual immigrant from the Caribbean island of Nevis, arrived in New York. He was deeply affected by the growing dissatisfaction with British rule among his fellow colonists. Hamilton was particularly impassioned by the idea that the American colonies deserved self-governance, free from foreign interference.

With the outbreak of the American Revolution in 1775, Hamilton's participation intensified. He initially joined a New York artillery company in 1776, quickly gaining recognition for his leadership skills. His articulate and powerful support for the revolutionary cause caught the attention of General George Washington, who, by 1777, appointed Hamilton as an aide-de-camp with the rank of Lieutenant Colonel on his personal staff.

Hamilton's military service featured pivotal moments, including the Battle of Trenton in December 1776. Despite harsh winter conditions, Hamilton played a significant role in the audacious crossing of the Delaware River, leading to a surprise victory that significantly boosted American troop morale.

The triumph at Trenton marked a turning point in the Revolution, highlighting the capability and resolve of the American army. Hamilton continued to serve with distinction throughout the war, contributing to several key victories, culminating in the decisive

Battle of Yorktown in 1781. The British surrender at Yorktown ultimately facilitated the conclusion of the conflict and the achievement of American independence.

Post-war, Hamilton redirected his energies toward the political reconstruction of the nation. He vigorously advocated for a strong federal government, playing a crucial role in addressing the inadequacies of the Articles of Confederation. As a principal architect of the Constitution, Hamilton significantly influenced the foundational framework of the United States.

Hamilton's wartime experiences profoundly shaped his political views. He recognized the necessity of a robust, centrally organized military and a resilient federal government, both essential to the survival and thriving of the new nation. His advocacy for these principles established him as a key figure in the Federalist Party.

Through his unwavering efforts during and after the war, Hamilton was instrumental in the fight for and establishment of American independence and governance. His vision for the United States constitutes a significant portion of his enduring legacy, continuing to influence the country long after his death.

Alexander Hamilton's unwavering dedication to the principles of liberty and governance exemplifies his pivotal role in the formation of the United States. His perseverance and strategic insight continue to inspire future generations.

Writing for the Cause

Alexander Hamilton, a young visionary committed to the American revolutionary cause, was profoundly influenced by the challenges the American colonies faced under British rule. Driven to make a meaningful impact, Hamilton leveraged his sharp intellect and exceptional writing skills to articulate his perspectives and arguments effectively.

One of Hamilton's most significant contributions was through his writings, especially in political advocacy. Among his most influential works were The Federalist Papers, which he co-authored with James

Madison and John Jay. These essays vigorously supported the adoption of the United States Constitution.

The Federalist Papers, consisting of 85 essays, aimed to explain and advocate for the ratification of the U.S. Constitution among New Yorkers and the wider public. Hamilton, who penned approximately 51 of these essays, provided compelling arguments for the necessity of a strong central government to ensure the nation's longevity and prosperity.

Hamilton's essays stood out for their clarity and depth. They addressed concerns about potential overreach by a robust central government and carefully explained the system of checks and balances designed to prevent any single branch from amassing excessive power. These essays were crucial in swaying public opinion and securing support for the Constitution.

Beyond The Federalist Papers, Hamilton wrote extensively to defend the Continental Congress and the efforts of the American Revolutionary War. His writings were vital in strengthening colonial resolve and unity during these tumultuous times.

Hamilton's exceptional ability to communicate complex ideas in a compelling and persuasive manner made his writings widely respected and influential. His contributions significantly advanced the cause of American liberty and governance.

As the first Secretary of the Treasury, Hamilton continued to use his writing skills to advocate for his economic policies. He vigorously defended his financial strategies, which included proposals for the federal government to assume state debts and the establishment of a national bank, clearly explaining their significance for a stable and thriving national economy.

Hamilton was also an eloquent speaker, and his oratory skills complemented his written advocacy. His dynamic public speaking engagements often reinforced the powerful arguments he presented in print, amplifying his influence in political discussions and policymaking.

Building a New Nation

Alexander Hamilton, a trusted aide to General George Washington during the American Revolutionary War, played a pivotal role in shaping the nascent United States. After the colonies declared independence from Great Britain, the pressing task was to establish a stable government to guide the nation forward.

Although Hamilton was not among the drafters of the United States Constitution, his influence was pronounced during its formation. As a delegate at the Constitutional Convention in Philadelphia in 1787, he collaborated with key figures like James Madison and Benjamin Franklin to debate and design the new government's structure.

Recognized for his sharp intellect and foresight, Hamilton was instrumental in advocating for a strong central government, distributing power among three branches: legislative (Congress), executive (the President), and judicial (the courts). He believed that this structure was crucial to unifying the diverse states and protecting national interests.

Following the Constitution's drafting, Hamilton, James Madison, and John Jay penned the Federalist Papers. This series of 85 essays significantly influenced the ratification of the Constitution by elucidating and advocating for its provisions.

In the Federalist Papers, Hamilton particularly championed a robust central government that would ensure stability and maintain checks and balances, which were vital for garnering public support for ratification.

Upon the inauguration of the new government, George Washington appointed Hamilton as the first Secretary of the Treasury. This role charged him with establishing a strong financial foundation for the country.

Hamilton introduced groundbreaking financial policies, such as the establishment of a national bank, which laid the foundations for a strong national economy. He advocated for the federal assumption of state debts from the Revolutionary War and placed taxes to fund these debts. Despite opposition from those wary of a powerful federal government, Hamilton's policies were instrumental in stabilizing the early American economy.

His efforts culminated in 1791 with the creation of the First Bank of the United States, which stabilized the economy by managing the government's fiscal transactions and issuing stable currency. This institution was crucial for economic standardization and growth during America's early years.

Beyond economic policies, Hamilton significantly shaped the United States' foreign policy. He advocated for prudent diplomatic relations and supported a strong military, ensuring that the young nation could assert and protect its international interests.

Alexander Hamilton's contributions were profound across multiple fronts—from constitutional foundations and fiscal strategies to diplomatic and military frameworks. His extensive contributions were pivotal in steering the United States toward its recognition as a resilient nation today.

Retreating from Politics

After serving as Secretary of the Treasury under President George Washington, Alexander Hamilton became embroiled in numerous political controversies, ultimately leading to his withdrawal from active political engagement.

By 1795, Hamilton's influence within the Federalist Party was waning as his policies and decisions faced increasing scrutiny and opposition.

Hamilton's situation deteriorated further in 1797. Backed into a corner, Hamilton employed a highly unconventional and risky strategy to protect his political legacy by making a public confession to clarify his actions and refute allegations of corruption or misuse of government funds. His admission was made through the "Reynolds Pamphlet," published in 1797, in which he detailed personal indiscretions but refuted claims of financial mismanagement.

Contrary to Hamilton's expectations, the pamphlet did not restore his reputation. Instead, the public confession led to a backlash, with many viewing it as an exhibition of poor judgment. His political adversaries leveraged this opportunity to further erode his credibility and standing.

As his influence waned and his reputation suffered, Hamilton gradually withdrew from active politics. He resigned from his position as Major General in the militia in 1800, a role to which he had been reappointed in 1798 after stepping down as Secretary of the Treasury in 1795. After exiting politics, Hamilton returned to his legal practice in New York City. His astute legal acumen ensured his success, and he handled numerous high-profile cases.

Despite the demands of his career, Hamilton was a dedicated family man. He and his wife, Elizabeth Schuyler Hamilton, had eight children. He cherished the time spent with his family and actively participated in their upbringing, striving to provide for them.

Even though he stepped back from the political limelight, Hamilton's passion for public service and national affairs never waned. He continued to write extensively, producing essays and commentaries on significant issues, illustrating his enduring commitment to America's future.

Hamilton's withdrawal from the political arena allowed him to reflect on his past actions and focus on personal growth and family. It also provided him time to consolidate his thoughts and contributions to the nation, maintaining his intellectual engagement until his tragic death in a duel in 1804. This period of reduced political involvement was a time of personal restoration and intellectual activity, preparing him for the influential roles he would still play in shaping American policies and institutions.

Despite his retreat from active politics, Hamilton's foundational contributions to the financial and political frameworks of the United States left an indelible mark on the developing nation.

A Founding Father's Feud

Alexander Hamilton was a brilliant and influential figure in American history, known for his forthright and assertive demeanor. These traits were particularly evident during his intense rivalry with Aaron Burr, another prominent figure of their time.

The discord between Hamilton and Burr escalated during the election of 1800. As a devout Federalist, Hamilton opposed Burr, a Democratic-Republican, for the role of U.S. President. Doubting Burr's integrity and fearing his ambitions, Hamilton endorsed Thomas Jefferson, which contributed significantly to Burr's loss, relegating him to the role of Vice President.

Feeling wronged by Hamilton's interference and public criticisms, Burr's resentment deepened when he ran for the governorship of New York in 1804. Again, Hamilton's public opposition played a crucial role in Burr's defeat in this election.

Furious and feeling his honor had been slighted, Burr challenged Hamilton to a duel—an accepted, though illegal, practice of their time for settling personal disputes. The duel took place on July 11, 1804, in Weehawken, New Jersey.

With great reluctance, Hamilton participated in the duel, feeling that his personal honor was at stake. Although he purportedly aimed to miss Burr intentionally by firing his pistol into the air, Burr's shot fatally wounded Hamilton, leading to his death the following day.

Hamilton's death was a pivotal event that drew widespread attention and sorrow. The duel highlighted the dangers of such confrontations and profoundly affected public perception of dueling.

Burr's political career suffered greatly after the duel. He was charged with murder but was later acquitted. Nevertheless, his reputation sustained irreversible damage, resulting in his political and social downfall.

Conversely, Hamilton's legacy as a founding father and a prominent intellect of the American Revolutionary period was cemented after his death. He is celebrated for his substantial contributions to the establishment of the United States' financial, political, and legal frameworks. His life, filled with both achievements and controversies, remains an intriguing chapter in American history.

While Hamilton's feud with Burr is often recalled for its dramatic end, it also exemplifies Hamilton's unwavering dedication to his principles and his transformative influence on American society, despite personal risks.

The Duel in Weehawken

Alexander Hamilton, a founding father of the United States, had numerous political adversaries, with one of the most prominent being Aaron Burr, then Vice President. Their prolonged political and personal conflicts culminated in a duel—a common yet dangerous method of that era for defending one's honor.

On the morning of July 11, 1804, the duel occurred in Weehawken, New Jersey, directly across the Hudson River from New York City. Adhering to dueling customs, Hamilton and Burr faced each other, standing about ten paces apart. They turned, aimed, and prepared to shoot upon receiving the signal.

Historians debate who fired first. It is known, however, that Hamilton's shot missed Burr, possibly intentionally fired into the air. Burr's return shot struck Hamilton in the lower abdomen, above the right hip, severely damaging his internal organs and lodging in his spine.

Severely wounded, Hamilton was transported back to New York City for medical attention. Despite the doctors' best efforts, he succumbed to his injuries and died on the afternoon of July 12, 1804, at the age of 49.

The duel also had grave consequences for Burr. Although not charged with murder in New York or New Jersey, his reputation suffered immensely. He became a polarizing figure in American politics, and his career never fully recovered. Later, Burr faced charges of treason in an unrelated case but was acquitted.

The death of Alexander Hamilton deeply affected the nation, mourning him as a pivotal architect of the U.S. financial system and a fervent advocate of the U.S. Constitution.

The duel stands as a stark reminder of how honor disputes, fueled by anger and pride, can lead to heartbreak. It also underscores the dangerous nature of dueling, a practice that was eventually renounced as societies sought more civilized ways to handle conflicts.

Despite the tragic end, Alexander Hamilton's legacy lives on, and he is celebrated for his significant role in shaping American governmental and financial frameworks.

Legacy of a Statesman

Alexander Hamilton, a brilliant Founding Father, and influential political figure, left a powerful legacy that continues to influence the United States.

As the first Secretary of the Treasury, Hamilton's significant contributions included establishing a robust financial system for the nation. This system included creating a national bank to strengthen the economy, promote trade, and ensure stability and growth.

Hamilton played a pivotal role in shaping the United States Constitution. Representing

New York at the Constitutional Convention, he advocated for a strong central government and emphasized checks and balances to protect individual rights.

His support for a centralized government was further showcased through his contributions to the Federalist Papers. Writing with James Madison and John Jay, Hamilton crafted essays that persuasively argued for the Constitution's ratification, securing support for the new government structure.

Hamilton's leadership extended to his military role during the American Revolutionary War. Serving as General George Washington's aide-de-camp, he was instrumental in the victories at the Battles of Trenton and Yorktown, significantly advancing American independence.

Hamilton's impact also permeates the U.S. legal system. In "Federalist No. 78," he championed an independent judiciary and the concept of judicial review. He argued that courts should have the power to review and void unconstitutional laws, reinforcing the checks and balances that define American democracy today.

Beyond his political and legal contributions, Hamilton envisioned America as a land of opportunity. He championed education, entrepreneurship, and hard work as means to transform individual lives and elevate the nation. His commitment to economic growth and innovation laid the foundations for America's status as an economic powerhouse.

Although Hamilton's life ended in a duel with Aaron Burr, his legacy endures. His financial policies and advocacy for a robust

Constitution continue to shape the United States, illustrating the profound impact one individual can have on a nation. His story exemplifies the power of determination, intelligence, and lasting influence.

Hamilton on Broadway

Alexander Hamilton, a pivotal figure in American history, lived over 200 years ago yet continues to inspire. His life is dramatically retold in the critically acclaimed Broadway musical, "Hamilton."

Created by Lin-Manuel Miranda, the musical debuted on Broadway in 2015, capturing the public's imagination. It narrates Alexander Hamilton's journey from his early days in the Caribbean to his significant role as one of the Founding Fathers of the United States.

A key factor in the musical's widespread appeal is its innovative fusion of historical narrative with hip-hop music. This unique approach not only engages audiences but also makes the historical events accessible and relatable through catchy tunes and compelling lyrics.

"Hamilton" encapsulates major events and themes from the American Revolution and the early years of the Republic, presenting complex historical details through the engaging medium of a musical. It highlights the political, social, and personal challenges faced by early American leaders.

The musical is renowned for its dynamic performances, with a talented cast bringing historical figures like Hamilton to life with vibrancy and depth. These performances significantly enhance the impact of the narrative on stage.

"Hamilton" has earned numerous accolades, including 11 Tony Awards, such as Best Musical, and the 2016 Pulitzer Prize for Drama. Its profound influence extends across theater and cultural discussions.

The musical has particularly resonated with younger audiences. Schools across America have embraced its music and themes as educational tools, making the learning process more engaging for students.

The success of "Hamilton" has not only boosted interest in Alexander Hamilton as a historical figure but also increased attendance at museums and historical sites related to his life and career.

Beyond the stage, "Hamilton" has stimulated discussions about the legacies of the Founding Fathers and the formation of the

United States. This engagement has been further enhanced by the musical's availability on streaming services and its use in educational settings.

In summary, "Hamilton" on Broadway has revolutionized how audiences engage with history. By blending entertainment with education, it has sparked a renewed interest in American history and celebrated the enduring legacy of Alexander Hamilton.

Family

Hamilton married Elizabeth Schuyler on December 14, 1780. Elizabeth came from a wealthy and influential New York family. The couple had eight children: Philip, Angelica, Alexander Jr., James Alexander, John Church, William Stephen, Eliza, and another Philip, named after his older brother who died in a duel in 1801.

Throughout his career, Hamilton was a devoted family man, although his extensive public service commitments often kept him away from home. He held significant roles, including that of Secretary of the Treasury, and also worked as an attorney.

Tragedy struck once more when Alexander Hamilton died on July 12, 1804, a day after his duel with Aaron Burr, which left him grievously wounded. His widow, Elizabeth, faced with raising a large family alone, became a dedicated steward of her husband's legacy. She lived to the age of 97, passing away in 1854, and spent much of her later life organizing Alexander's papers and advocating for public causes, notably establishing New York City's first private orphanage.

Influence

Alexander Hamilton was not only a pivotal figure in the founding of the United States; his influence still shapes our nation's government, economy, and legal system. This section explores some key aspects of Hamilton's enduring legacy.

Hamilton's influence on our country is most notable through his contributions to the Constitution. As a principal author of the Federalist Papers, he argued vigorously for a strong central government and the necessity of a written constitution. These writings played a crucial role in securing the

Constitution's ratification, profoundly affecting the structure and function of the federal government as we know it today.

His economic policies also had a significant impact. As the first Secretary of the Treasury, Hamilton established the nation's financial architecture, which included the creation of a national bank, the implementation of tariffs, and a system for managing the national debt. These measures stabilized the fledgling economy of the United States and laid the foundations for its future growth and development.

Hamilton's vision for a strong, unified nation deeply influenced the political landscape of early America. His staunch advocacy for a powerful federal government helped forge a robust framework that underpins the modern American state. His ideas were crucial during a formative period when the balance of power between state and federal authorities was being defined.

In the legal realm, Hamilton's contributions were equally substantial. His experiences and achievements as a lawyer helped shape several fundamental aspects of the American legal system. His legal philosophy and practice influenced his contemporaries and continue to inform modern legal discourse.

Hamilton's perspectives on immigration also hold lasting relevance. He saw immigration as a means to enrich and strengthen the nation, a viewpoint that still influences contemporary debates and policies on immigration in the United States.

Alexander Hamilton's impact is apparent in various facets of modern-day America. His innovative ideas on government structure, economic policies, legal frameworks, and immigration continue to resonate and shape American society. Delving into Hamilton's life and works offers invaluable insights into the foundational principles that have both shaped and continue to guide the United States.

Exploring Hamilton's Work

Throughout his life, Alexander Hamilton distinguished himself with an unwavering work ethic and pivotal contributions to the founding of the United States. This chapter explores some of his most significant achievements.

Hamilton's most influential role was as the first Secretary of the Treasury, where he played a critical part in shaping the nation's financial framework. A staunch advocate for a strong central government, he implemented key measures to stabilize and fortify the national economy.

Recognizing the importance of a robust banking system, Hamilton championed the establishment of the First Bank of the United States. This institution aimed to provide a stable currency and manage the nation's finances. Despite substantial opposition, he successfully persuaded Congress to authorize its creation in 1791.

Hamilton also made significant contributions during the Constitutional Convention. While he had limited involvement in drafting the United States Constitution, his participation in the convention and subsequent efforts were vital in establishing a robust federal government.

His intellectual prowess shone brightly in his contributions to the Federalist Papers. Alongside James Madison and John Jay, Hamilton wrote persuasive essays advocating for the Constitution's ratification, shaping the views of both skeptics and supporters.

In addition to his political endeavors, Hamilton was prominent in the legal field. He resumed his legal practice in New York City after the Revolutionary War, handling several notable cases. This facet of his career not only showcased his legal expertise but also underscored his dedication to public service.

As Secretary of the Treasury, Hamilton undertook the monumental task of establishing the nation's creditworthiness. His strategies included the federal assumption of state debts incurred during the Revolutionary War, which was crucial in bolstering national financial credibility. Furthermore, he introduced tariffs and excise taxes to increase government revenue.

The impact of Hamilton's efforts in creating a powerful central government and a resilient financial system is profound. His visionary policies laid the foundation for the United States' future growth and prosperity, marking his lasting influence on American fiscal policy and governmental structure.

Alexander Hamilton's tenure as Secretary of the Treasury, his influential advocacy for the U.S. Constitution, and his distinguished legal career are lasting testaments to his dedication and impact on the nation. His visionary ideas and policies continue to resonate in contemporary discussions about governmental and economic practices in the U.S., emphasizing his critical role in American history.

Dueling Code

Alexander Hamilton, a distinguished American Founding Father, held multiple roles, including that of economist and politician. Despite his vast expertise and accomplishments, Hamilton is often recalled for his adherence to a common practice of his era—dueling. Dueling, a method to resolve disputes and defend honor, was governed by a structured set of regulations known as the "dueling code."

Contrary to chaotic or lawless perceptions, dueling was highly regulated with strict guidelines. Participants, referred to as duelists, were required to follow these rules to ensure the duel was conducted in a socially acceptable manner.

A critical rule involved the appointment of a "second"—a trusted individual chosen by each duelist. The second played an essential role by negotiating terms with the opponent's second and striving to amicably settle the dispute before any gunfire.

Weapon selection was also pivotal, with pistols being the preferred choice. Duelists had to mutually agree on the type of weapons used, which promoted fairness and an even contest.

According to the dueling code, duelists would stand at a predetermined distance, often marked by their seconds. The duel would commence with a typical signal, such as the drop of a handkerchief by one of the seconds. Participants would then take turns to fire their weapons.

The code provided opportunities for reconciliation after the first exchange of gunfire. If no fatal wounds had been inflicted, the seconds could intervene to negotiate peace, potentially concluding the duel without further violence.

This code was adhered to during the unfortunate duel between Alexander Hamilton and Aaron Burr on July 11, 1804, in Weehawken, New Jersey. In this encounter, both men fired their weapons; however, Hamilton was struck and succumbed to his injuries the next day. Burr's fatal shot not only ended Hamilton's life but also marked a pivotal moment that intensified the growing opposition to dueling in America.

The aftermath of Hamilton's death significantly influenced the perception of dueling in American society. Over the following years, dueling experienced a considerable decline and was progressively outlawed throughout the nation.

Although Alexander Hamilton's involvement in the duel constitutes a relatively minor part of his extensive legacy, it provides valuable insight into the cultural and social norms of his time. It underscores the complexities of honor, conflict resolution, and the repercussions of adhering to societal expectations of the era.

Financial Vision

Alexander Hamilton, a prominent statesman and leading economist, played a pivotal role in shaping the economic framework of the United States. As the first Secretary of the Treasury, his vision focused on establishing a strong and stable economy essential for the nation's growth and sustainability.

Hamilton faced the monumental challenge of managing the substantial debt incurred by the United States during the Revolutionary War. Owing significant amounts to both domestic creditors and foreign nations, he recognized the critical need for fiscal responsibility. To stabilize the nation's finances and establish international credibility and reliability, Hamilton introduced his "Report on Public Credit" to Congress in 1790. His plan proposed that the federal government assume the states' war debts and finance these through the issuance of new securities. Consolidating these debts under the national government aimed to enhance the country's creditworthiness and reassure investors of their reliability.

Another fundamental aspect of Hamilton's strategy was the establishment of a national bank. He advocated for the creation of the First Bank of the United States, which would serve both as a federal depository and a creditor for state projects, thus providing a stable national currency. The bank was designed to be a robust institution capable of supporting commercial and governmental financial needs.

However, Hamilton's proposal faced considerable opposition from advocates of a decentralized federal structure, who feared the national bank would centralize too much power with the federal government. Despite these concerns, Hamilton successfully argued that the bank was essential for managing the nation's finances and fell within the constitutional powers of the federal government. As a result, in 1791, Congress established the First Bank of the United States.

Furthermore, Hamilton supported protective tariffs and the encouragement of domestic industries. He believed these economic policies would decrease dependence on foreign goods and stimulate the growth of local industries, thereby enhancing economic independence and development.

Hamilton's economic strategies ignited vigorous debates and were not universally embraced. His advocacy for a strong central government and proactive economic policies, however, laid significant foundations for future U.S. economic policy. Despite controversies and opposition, many of Hamilton's principles, such as the importance of a robust financial system and support for domestic manufacturing, continue to influence American economic policies today.

Through his visionary financial strategies, Alexander Hamilton made an immense contribution to building a stable and prosperous economic foundation for the United States, the effects of which are still evident.

Hamilton and the Constitution

Alexander Hamilton was instrumental in the creation of the United States Constitution. As one of the Founding Fathers, his substantial contributions shaped the design and facilitated the ratification of this crucial document.

Following the American Revolution, the United States struggled with the weaknesses of the Articles of Confederation, which lacked the centralized power necessary for effective governance. Hamilton, advocating for a stronger federal government, viewed centralized power as crucial for national stability and prosperity.

In 1787, as a delegate at the Constitutional Convention in Philadelphia, Hamilton played a significant role despite having less influence than some others on the Constitution's final form. He was a staunch supporter of a powerful executive branch, the establishment of a bicameral legislature, and a judiciary to interpret laws.

Hamilton's most significant contributions came through "The Federalist Papers," a series of 85 essays he co-authored with James Madison and John Jay. Writing 51 of these essays himself, Hamilton was pivotal in explaining and defending the Constitution to the public, which was crucial for gaining its ratification support.

Hamilton regarded the Constitution as a framework designed to protect individual rights while ensuring economic stability and national growth. He championed a clear rule of law and a checks and balances system to prevent power abuses.

Despite facing considerable opposition, Hamilton's vision of a strong central government came to fruition with the Constitution's ratification in 1788 and subsequent implementation. His influence continued as he became the first Secretary of the Treasury under President George Washington.

In this role, Hamilton laid the foundation for the nation's financial system, supporting the creation of a national bank and promoting industrial and commercial growth. These policies, though initially met with controversy, were essential in solidifying the economic structure of the emerging United States.

Alexander Hamilton's lasting impact on the U.S. Constitution highlights his vision for a robust federal government capable of managing a complex national economy and protecting individual freedoms. His legacy underscores the importance of active and informed citizenship, elucidates the power of well-crafted ideas, and reaffirms the Constitution's continuous relevance in American governance.

Leadership

Alexander Hamilton was a visionary leader whose initiatives played a crucial role in shaping the nascent United States. His leadership style, characterized by intelligence, purpose, and innovative strategies, significantly impacted various domains, including the military, finance, politics, and social reforms.

Military Leadership

During the Revolutionary War, Hamilton began his military career as an artillery officer and later advanced to become a senior aide to General George Washington. Renowned for his tactical expertise and bravery, Hamilton's military career reached its pinnacle with a decisive assault at the Siege of Yorktown in 1781, which played a vital role in securing American victory.

Political and Financial Leadership

Post-war, Hamilton transitioned into politics and emerged as a pivotal figure at the Constitutional Convention in 1787. Contrary to some delegates who favored strong state governments, Hamilton championed a robust central government, which he deemed essential for national stability and economic growth.

As the first Secretary of the Treasury, Hamilton implemented a series of audacious financial strategies. He founded the First Bank of the United States in 1791 to stabilize and strengthen the national economy. His strategies included the federal assumption of state debts and establishing a system to collect customs duties and excise taxes.

Contributions to Law and Media

Hamilton also profoundly influenced the spheres of law and media. He was instrumental in establishing the Federalist Party and co-authored "The Federalist Papers," a collection of 85 essays advocating for the ratification of the U.S. Constitution. These essays greatly influenced the philosophical underpinnings of American governance.

Social Initiatives

In addition to his political and financial endeavors, Hamilton championed social causes. He played a significant role in the New York Manumission Society, which pushed for the abolition of slavery.

Legacy

Hamilton's advocacy for a strong central government and a dynamic economy profoundly influenced America's trajectory toward becoming a stable and thriving nation. His policies set the groundwork for the U.S. financial system, and his support for federal governance continues to influence American political frameworks.

The Broadway musical "Hamilton" has popularized his contributions, portraying his journey from an immigrant to a revolutionary leader and prominent statesman. The musical has reignited interest in Hamilton's seminal role in American history, highlighting his extensive leadership and lasting legacy.

Legal Career

Alexander Hamilton's legal career began after the American Revolution and had a significant impact on the young nation. His sharp intellect and passion for justice shaped the legal landscape.

Hamilton studied and practiced law in New York City, where he gained a reputation for his intellectual prowess and persuasive oratory. Admitted to the bar in 1783, he became authorized to practice law in New York courts.

In a notable case, Rutgers v. Waddington (1784), Hamilton represented Joshua

Waddington against Elizabeth Rutgers, a wealthy widow seeking damages from the British occupation of New York City. Hamilton argued that the Trespass Act should not apply retroactively, as the British occupation was lawful under wartime regulations. This case was pivotal in establishing the rule of law in America, particularly in relation to actions committed under previous governance.

Hamilton's legal pursuits intertwined with his political ambitions. As a member of the New York State Assembly and later as a delegate to the Constitutional Convention, he played a crucial role in standardizing and refining the state's legal system. His focus was on establishing a fair and efficient judiciary grounded in justice and due process.

In addition to his practice, Hamilton wrote legal opinions and essays that contributed to the foundation of critical legal principles. His writings showcased both persuasive legal arguments and a profound understanding of constitutional principles.

Although not as renowned as his contributions to finance and politics, Hamilton's legal career laid the groundwork for the United States legal system. His dedication to justice and the rule of law continues to influence the legal profession and American jurisprudence.

Hamilton used his legal expertise to advocate for a fair and just system, viewing it as vital to the nation's success and prosperity. His contributions underscore the significance of justice and equity in the ongoing pursuit of a more perfect union.

Spanning years and encompassing a diverse array of cases and legal writings, Hamilton's legacy in law reminds us of the pivotal role a just legal system plays in achieving a more perfect union.

Views on Immigration

Alexander Hamilton, a Founding Father of the United States, played a crucial role in shaping the country's financial system and governance. As an immigrant, he held progressive views on immigration, recognizing the significant contributions immigrants made to American society in its formative years.

Born on the Caribbean island of Nevis, Hamilton faced adversity early in life. He moved to the North American colonies in 1772, initially settling in New Jersey before continuing his education in New York. His own experiences endowed him with a deep understanding of the immigrant experience.

In New York, Hamilton's encounters with a diverse populace likely shaped his perception of America as a nation invigorated by the talents and energies of newcomers. He valued the skills and perspectives that immigrants brought to America.

While Hamilton's professional writings occasionally touched on immigration, they predominantly revealed a practical approach, considering the economic and social benefits that immigrants could offer. Notably, he advocated for attracting skilled workers to bolster America's economic prowess.

However, the often-cited quote attributing views on the "safety of a republic" to Hamilton actually reflects his concerns about national unity and identity rather than immigration itself. This underscores his broader apprehensions about foreign influence and the importance of national cohesion.

Despite Hamilton's overall favorable stance on immigration, it's important to acknowledge that his era was also characterized by skepticism towards immigration. Issues related to the assimilation of immigrants and their impact on American identity were part of a larger national dialogue.

On the policy front, the Naturalization Act of 1790, passed during Hamilton's tenure in Congress, set the first standardized rules for naturalized citizenship—requiring a two-year residency in the U.S. before eligibility. While Hamilton did not author this legislation, it reflected the structured approach he favored for integrating immigrants into society.

In conclusion, Alexander Hamilton perceived the United States as a land of opportunity. Both his personal and professional experiences support his belief in the substantial benefits that immigrants bring to the nation. Despite the era's challenges and complexities, Hamilton's advocacy for immigration forms an integral part of his vision for a robust and dynamic United States.

Reflecting on Hamilton's contributions offers key insights into the historical nuances of American immigration policy and its continual development. His personal background as an immigrant and his legislative actions underscore his enduring belief in the strength that diversity adds to the American mosaic.

Vision for America

Alexander Hamilton was a visionary whose ideas significantly shaped the foundation and early development of the United States. He envisioned America as a strong, unified, and economically robust nation guided by a powerful federal government.

Hamilton believed a strong central government was crucial in preventing chaos and ensuring unity. He argued that without such a government, individual states might prioritize their own interests, leading to conflicts and weakening the nation.

Hamilton proposed several key initiatives to solidify his vision. The establishment of the First Bank of the United States was a significant stride. He argued that a national bank was essential for stabilizing the nation's financial system, securing federal funds, facilitating business loans, and standardizing currency.

Hamilton's proposals faced significant opposition, particularly from figures like Thomas Jefferson, who advocated for stronger state governments rather than a predominant federal authority. This led to intense debates between Federalists and Anti-Federalists, reflecting contrasting visions for America's future.

Despite opposition, Hamilton's financial strategies were implemented with the support of President George Washington. The inauguration of the First Bank in 1791 was a pivotal moment in American fiscal policy, playing a crucial role in resolving the financial difficulties that followed the Revolutionary War.

Hamilton's plans also encompassed the development of manufacturing and industry. He supported protective tariffs to encourage industrial growth, endorsed government-funded infrastructure projects, and promoted foreign investments, diversifying the economic base and fostering early financial independence from European manufacturers.

Additionally, Hamilton recognized the importance of military strength and infrastructure. He supported the establishment of a standing army, a federal navy, and military academies to train officers, enhancing national defense and international standing.

Hamilton also placed a high value on education, viewing it as essential for civic empowerment and national strength. He championed initiatives such as the founding of the New York Manumission Society and its associated school, the African Free School, which educated children of slaves and free people of color.

While not directly responsible for founding New York City's first orphanage, his involvement in social issues underscored his broader concerns for societal welfare and structure.

Political Philosophy

Alexander Hamilton was a pivotal figure in the founding of the United States who played a crucial role in shaping the country's political philosophy. His influential ideas about government and its impact on citizens were essential during the nation's formative years.

Hamilton strongly advocated for a powerful central government, which he believed was necessary to maintain order and ensure prosperity. He envisaged a robust executive branch led by a president with sufficient authority to make critical decisions promptly, aiming for effective governance.

These views were a direct response to the weaknesses he perceived in the Articles of Confederation, which lacked strong federal control.

In terms of security, Hamilton supported a formidable military. Recognizing the importance of defense, he advocated for a permanent, well-trained army. Although some contemporaries feared that such a force could lead to tyranny, Hamilton considered it essential for national defense and deterring international threats.

On the economic front, Hamilton championed a strong financial infrastructure. He favored industrial and commercial growth, believing it was key to national prosperity. To support this, he advocated for the establishment of a national bank to stabilize and enhance the nation's financial health, thus facilitating economic development.

Education was another cornerstone of Hamilton's philosophy. He believed that a successful republic relied on an educated populace equipped to participate effectively in democratic processes. Hamilton supported initiatives that made education more accessible to a greater number of citizens, recognizing that well-informed individuals could make thoughtful contributions to governance.

Hamilton also emphasized the rule of law and the significance of a strong judiciary. He advocated for an independent judicial system capable of interpreting the Constitution impartially. This stance frequently placed him in opposition to Thomas Jefferson, who favored a more decentralized approach and a narrower interpretation of the Constitution.

The impact of Hamilton's political thought remains considerable. His advocacy for a strong central government, a dynamic economy, and an educated public continues to shape American governance. His comprehensive vision for the United States reflects both the challenges and aspirations of the nation during its early years.

Throughout his career, Hamilton's observations and experiences influenced his views on effective government. His efforts were driven by a commitment to establishing a framework that would support the prosperity and well-being of all citizens. Hamilton's legacy stands as a testament to his profound influence on the fundamental principles of the United States.

Role in the Revolution

Alexander Hamilton played a pivotal role in the American Revolution. At just 21 years old, he joined the fight for freedom against British rule.

Born in the Caribbean, Hamilton was passionately committed to the American cause for independence. With a sharp intellect and a strong desire to influence the conflict, he eagerly sought to contribute to revolutionary efforts.

Hamilton first engaged in the war as a captain of an artillery company. His leadership and bravery in battles like the

Battle of White Plains and the Battle of Princeton quickly led to his promotion to aide-de-camp.

As General George Washington's trusted aide-de-camp, Hamilton played a significant role. Serving as Washington's right-hand man, he functioned as an advisor, secretary, and confidant, remaining by Washington's side for much of the war, sharing in the challenges and triumphs alike.

Highly valued for his intelligence and strategic insights, Hamilton's counsel was crucial during key moments of the war, such as the Battle of Yorktown. There, Hamilton led an assault that was vital in securing a decisive victory against the British.

Hamilton demonstrated notable bravery in numerous engagements. For example, at the

Battle of Monmouth, he displayed exceptional courage and was instrumental in rallying the troops. He also took part in the daring crossing of the Delaware River, a maneuver that surprised the enemy and marked a turning point in the war.

During the harsh winter at Valley Forge, Hamilton tirelessly worked to improve conditions for the troops, showcasing his deep commitment to the revolutionary cause.

Beyond his military service, Hamilton also used his intellectual prowess to help shape the emerging nation. While he was not a member of the Continental Congress during the war, his political insights later played a role in the drafting of the Federalist Papers, which advocated for the ratification of the Constitution.

Throughout the revolution, Hamilton's strategic thinking, leadership qualities, and unwavering dedication were essential in securing independence. His journey from a young immigrant to an influential figure in the American Revolution is a testament to his commitment to the principles of liberty.

Hamilton's role during the revolution laid the groundwork for his later contributions as a statesman and Founding Father, where he continued to materialize his vision for a united and prosperous America.

Contributions to the Constitution

Alexander Hamilton, a founding father of the United States, played a pivotal role in shaping the U.S. Constitution. As an author of the Federalist Papers, he used his exceptional writing skills to argue for a strong central government, which he considered essential for the nation's survival and prosperity.

Hamilton pinpointed the frailties of the Articles of Confederation, the nation's first governing document, criticizing its lack of a robust federal framework needed for economic stability and defense. Alongside

James Madison and John Jay, he wrote numerous essays, grouped under The Federalist Papers, to strongly advocate for the ratification of the proposed Constitution. These essays systematically addressed and countered the objections of its detractors.

Distributed across the thirteen states, The Federalist Papers played a crucial role in swaying public opinion towards a more centralized government. Hamilton's detailed explanations within these papers elucidated the intentions of the Constitution and were instrumental in its ratification.

Through The Federalist Papers, Hamilton demonstrated a profound grasp of political theory, calling for a balanced federal system that would ensure stability, protect individual rights, and unify the states. His vision particularly resonated with those concerned about the nation's international reputation and internal unity.

The persuasive arguments presented in these essays helped secure the Constitution's ratification, with the required number of states endorsing the document by 1788, and it officially came into effect in 1789.

Furthermore, Hamilton's impact extended beyond his written works. Although he was not an official delegate, he participated actively in the Constitutional Convention of 1787 as part of the New York delegation. There, he advocated for a strong national government and a robust executive branch.

At the convention, Hamilton argued for a president endowed with significant powers, which are key to decisive leadership. This strong stance influenced the structure of the presidency as outlined in the Constitution.

Hamilton also championed lifetime appointments for federal judges to ensure an independent judiciary unaffected by political pressures. This principle was embedded into the Constitution and continues to be upheld today.

Alexander Hamilton's efforts were crucial in establishing a strong federal government. His visionary proposals during the Constitutional drafting and his influential writings not only shaped the executive branch but also promoted an independent judiciary. His integral yet often understated role at the Constitutional Convention and beyond underscore his enduring commitment to a robust, unified America.

Remembering Hamilton

Alexander Hamilton, a pivotal figure in the early formation of the American political system, remains a significant character in our historical narrative more than two centuries after his death. This chapter explores the various ways in which Hamilton's legacy continues to influence contemporary society.

Hamilton is honored through numerous monuments and memorials. A notable example is the Hamilton Grange National Memorial in New York City, the only house Hamilton ever owned. This site has been preserved as a museum, exhibiting his contributions to American society.

In addition to the Grange, statues of Hamilton stand in several cities across the United States, including Washington, D.C., and Chicago. These statues symbolize his critical role in shaping the nation.

Literature also preserves Hamilton's memory. Numerous biographies offer insights into his life, achievements, and the complexities of his character, enhancing our understanding of his impact on American history.

A contemporary homage to Hamilton's legacy is the Broadway musical "Hamilton," created by Lin-Manuel Miranda. By blending hip-hop with traditional musical styles, the show has not only popularized Hamilton's story but also captivated a diverse audience, introducing many young people to his historical significance.

Hamilton's ideas, particularly in economic policy, continue to be influential. His advocacy for a strong central government and the establishment of a national bank are crucial for understanding today's financial systems in the United States. His perspectives on these topics remain subjects of discussion among economists and historians.

The legacy of Alexander Hamilton is also cherished by his descendants. Hamilton and his wife, Elizabeth Schuyler, had eight children. Their descendants actively honor his memory and contribute to the preservation and dissemination of his historical importance.

Thus, Hamilton's memory is celebrated and studied through monuments, literature, music, his transformative ideas, and his direct descendants. His life and works offer enduring lessons, inspiring ongoing debate and admiration among scholars, leaders, and citizens alike.

CONCLUSION

As we reach the conclusion of Alexander Hamilton's remarkable journey, we are left to ponder the lasting impact of his life's work and the enduring questions that continue to echo through American history. From his early struggles on the island of Nevis to his influential role in the creation of the United States, Hamilton's story is one of relentless ambition, intellectual prowess, and an unwavering vision for the future.

Hamilton's legacy is woven into the very fabric of the nation he helped to build. His contributions to the Constitution, his visionary economic policies, and his fervent advocacy for a strong central government have left an indelible mark on the American political and economic landscape. The institutions he established, such as the national bank, and the principles he championed, like federalism and fiscal responsibility, continue to influence contemporary debates and shape the direction of the country.

But beyond his public achievements, Hamilton's personal story of resilience and determination serves as an inspiration. Despite facing abandonment, poverty, and personal loss, he rose to prominence through sheer force of will and intellectual brilliance. His life exemplifies the spirit of the American dream, the belief that hard work and talent can overcome any obstacle.

The controversies and conflicts that marked Hamilton's career also offer valuable lessons. His fierce rivalries with figures like Thomas Jefferson and Aaron Burr, as well as the scandals that marred his reputation, highlight the complexities of human nature and the challenges of public life. These episodes remind us that greatness often comes with flaws and that the pursuit of ideals can be fraught with personal and political peril.

In the end, Alexander Hamilton's story is a testament to the power of ideas and the impact of individuals on the course of history. His vision for America—a nation built on innovation, economic strength, and a robust federal system—continues to resonate and inspire. As we reflect on his life and legacy, we are reminded that the challenges and debates of Hamilton's time are not so different from those we face today. His contributions to the American experiment endure, offering guidance and inspiration for future generations.

As we close this book, let us carry forward the lessons of Alexander Hamilton's life: the importance of resilience in the face of adversity, the power of visionary thinking, and the enduring value of dedication to public service. Hamilton's legacy is not just a chapter in history but a living influence that continues to shape the nation and inspire those who strive to build a better future.